PRAYERS FOR PURPOSE

A 30-Day Devotional Journal for the **Purpose-Driven Woman**

ARIKA DAVENPORT

Prayers for Purpose-A 30 Day Devotional Journal for the Purpose-Driven Woman
Copyright © 2020 by Arika Davenport

All Rights Reserved. Published 2020. Scriptures taken from the Holy Bible, New International Version®, NIV®. Copyright © 1973, 1978, 1984, 2011 by Biblica, Inc.™ Used by permission of Zondervan. All rights reserved worldwide. www.zondervan.com The "NIV" and "New International Version" are trademarks registered in the United States Patent and Trademark Office by Biblica, Inc.™. Scripture taken from the New King James Version®. Copyright © 1982 by Thomas Nelson. Used by permission. All rights reserved. Scripture quotations marked (AMP) are taken from the Amplified Bible, Copyright © 1954, 1958, 1962, 1964, 1965, 1987 by The Lockman Foundation. Used by permission.

No part of this publication may be reproduced, distributed, or transmitted in any form or by any means, including photocopying, recording, or other electronic or mechanical methods, without the prior written permission of the publisher, except in the case of brief quotations embodied in critical reviews and certain other noncommercial uses permitted by copyright law. For permission requests, write to the publisher, addressed "Attention: Permissions Coordinator," at the address below.

First published by She Pursues Purpose LLC
ISBN 978-0-578-85361-1

Printed in the United States of America

She Pursues Purpose LLC
P.O. Box 842
Pickerington, OH 43147
Shepursuespurpose.com

(Christian, Devotional, Journal)

To my sons, Aaron & Adon
I pray that every step you take is toward the purpose God has for you. Being your mom has been the greatest blessing from God above all else. I love you both!

To my mom, resting in Heaven
I know you are smiling down and watching over us. Thank you for teaching me how to be a strong, determined, and independent woman. May the work you've done speak for you.

To every woman who has trusted me to mentor, coach, support, and pray for you
Thank you for every time you hit reply, for every time you show up, for every time you encourage me. You asked for a book, so I answered. To every single sister in purpose, who joined the Pray for Purpose challenge, this is for you.

To my husband, my love and my friend
Thank you for your support, your encouragement and doing this thing called life with me. I love you so much.

Contents

Pregnant with Purpose 1

Day 1 Prayer...He Already Knew 4

Day 2 Prayer...God Has a Plan for You #theblueprint 7

Day 3 Prayer...What Is Purpose? 10

Day 4 Prayer...You Have a Gift! 13

Day 5 Prayer...It's Just the Beginning! 16

Day 6 Prayer...I Mean, It's Whatever 19

Day 7 Prayer...Resting Is a Part of Working 23

Day 8 Prayer...This May Hurt a Little 27

Day 9 Prayer...Look Out for Haters 30

Day 10 Prayer...What Are You Asking For? 34

Day 11 Prayer...Ride the Waves 38

Day 12 Prayer...Wait for It 42

Day 13 Prayer...Umm, Lord, I Don't Know 46

Day 14 Prayer...One Size Doesn't Fit All 50

Day 15 Prayer Don't Stop! Run Your Race! 54

Day 16 Prayer...I Just Want to See You Win 58

Day 17 Prayer...See It with Your Pen 62

Day 18 Prayer…If Only You Knew 66

Day 19 Prayer...Crumb Fed 70

Day 20 Prayer...Just a Little More 74

Day 21 Prayer...Prepare for the Promises 78

Day 22 Prayer...Purpose in Your Pain 82

Day 23 Prayer...What's My Name? 85

Day 24 Prayer...What Is the Number? 89

Day 25 Prayer...Don't Put All Your Eggs in One Basket 92

Day 26 Prayer...How Bad Do You Want It? 96

Day 27 Prayer...Let's Get Ready to Rumble! 100

Day 28 Prayer...A Recipe for You 104

Day 29 Prayer...The Chosen One 109

Day 30 Prayer…To Know Him Is to Love Him 113

A Letter to My Sister in Purpose 117

What Is My Purpose? 120

Pregnant with Purpose

Lord, what is my purpose? What can I do?

I found myself asking God those questions around January 2018. In spite of obtaining a master's degree, getting married, buying a house, and becoming a great mother and wife, I was lost. I had lost who I was as a woman and as an individual. I was so busy in my roles that I neglected myself as a person. Although I didn't want to seem ungrateful, I knew there was more to me. I entered a season of feeling unfulfilled and discontent. No matter how hard I tried to ignore it, I felt a nudge. I sensed a pull toward something more, but I didn't know what that was or where to start.

So I did what any purpose-seeking woman would do.

I went on a spiritual retreat, right inside my home. I committed to prayer, studying the Word, self-development, and personal growth. I attended events that inspired me, I read books on purpose, I listened to sermons, and I did everything I could to feed that starving purpose pain on the inside of me. I meditated on 1 Corinthians 12 about the different spiritual gifts and asked God what I could do that would benefit the body of Christ.

One day, it clicked.

Although I would like to say I had this mountaintop, Moses-type encounter with God, I didn't. One day, it just clicked. I realized that during my own pursuit of purpose, God had prepared me to equip and empower women like you to pursue their purpose. My personal and professional experiences were all pieces to my purpose puzzle. God has an amazing way of making things make sense!

I went into labor, and unto us a child was born.

My pregnancy was the pursuit of my purpose. Although I wasn't sure what it would look like in the beginning, I pushed out my purpose and She Pursues Purpose was born. It started off as a blog but quickly transformed into a movement, an assignment, a call from God. I created She Purposes Purpose to help women across the world discover their path to purpose and deliver their gifts to the world without neglecting their family or themselves.

Lights, camera, action!

I'm an introvert, yet God wanted me to be a front-liner and deliver purpose to his daughters. In spite of being nervous and shy, I obeyed. Since starting She Pursues Purpose, I have been featured on award-winning podcasts and seminars, educating women about purpose. Through my Purpose Partner Program, I have helped women walk in purpose. I have learned to do it afraid. I mastered being comfortable with being uncomfortable, and I am changing lives every single day.

You are pregnant with purpose too.

I share my story because I had the same objections and doubts you've probably had at some point. Even when I knew purpose was my lane, I questioned the call before I fully answered it. I want you to know that no matter where you are in your purpose journey, there is more. Your purpose is always growing, developing, and evolving inside you. Purpose isn't something you find; it's not lost. It is something you discover. Purpose is right in your belly, right on the inside. You may not know the gender, you may not have a name for it yet, but, friend, you are pregnant with purpose. My prayer is that you discover everything God has placed inside you.

If you need a purpose partner...

I am a firm believer that purpose cannot be achieved alone. God demonstrated this in the Bible. Everything God wanted to accomplish on earth was accomplished through a human. Although He could've done everything on His own, He chose to use women like Mary, Esther, and Ruth to carry out his plans. He knew the importance of partnerships. If you are looking for a community, a support system, a tribe of purpose-driven women, let's connect on Instagram or Facebook @shepursuespurpose. I offer tons of support, resources, and inspiration for the purpose-driven woman. Visit she-pursues-purpose.ck.page/affirmations to receive a free downloadable *Power of I Am Affirmations* gift.

Before I formed you in the womb I knew you, before you were born I set you apart. — Jeremiah 1:5, NIV

He Already Knew

Did you know before you were even born God knew you? *Before* He divinely ordered your mother's steps, *before* He decided when and how you would be born, God said He wanted you! He determined beforehand everything about you—how you would look, your personality, your strengths, your weaknesses, and your passion and gifts. Before He began the detailed and amazing process of conception and birth, *He knew you.*

God decided in advance *why* He would create you *(your purpose)* and then He created you. *You were created for a purpose and with a purpose.* Everything you have been through in life, the good, the bad, and the ugly, is connected to His purpose for you. God set you apart for a reason. You are not an accident or a mistake. You were created with intent! It's not His will for you to "fit in." Be who God created you to be. No one can do you better than you.

Purpose Prayer for Today

Father God, thank You for knowing me before I even knew myself. Thank You, Lord, that even if I don't fully know the purpose for which You created me, I still have one, and it's only a matter of time before I walk in it. Thank You that I don't have be like anyone else because You created me just how You wanted me to be. Lord, show me clearly the purpose you have formed inside me. Let me recognize it and pursue it like never before. Thank You for accepting me as I am. I declare today I am set apart to walk in my purpose and give You the glory! In Jesus's name, Amen.

Day 1

Have you ever felt like you didn't fit in? Do you ever wonder why you are the way you are? Are you willing to embrace who God created you to be? Are you willing to do the things God created you to do? How can you fully accept who you are and use that to glorify God and help others?

_____

_____

_____

_____

_____

_____

_____

_____

_____

_____

_____

_____

Daily Affirmation: I am who God says I am, and I will do what God created me to do.

Day 2 Prayer

"For I know the plans I have for you," declares the Lord, *"plans to prosper you and not to harm you, plans to give you hope and a future."* —Jeremiah 29:11, NIV

God Has a Plan for You #theblueprint

One thing I have learned about God is that He sees the end of a thing before He even starts the beginning. Before He ever said, "Let there be," He already had a plan for how He would create the whole universe. He didn't just randomly decide one day to create the world. He had already configured a seven-day blueprint with every detail laid out for Creation.

Often, we worry about things God never intended us to worry about. God said He knows the plans He has for you. If God created Creation in seven days (and clearly you were part of that Creation), may I submit to you that He also has a blueprint laid out for your life?

A blueprint is a detailed and precise design or drawing. It is very particular as to timing, measurements, and positions. God promises in His word that *His blueprint for your life leads to prosperity, protection, hope, and a good future!* Do you receive that? When you allow God to be the head and the master architect of your life, you qualify for His blueprint. Nothing happens by chance. Nothing happens out of His timing. It's all part of His plan. Allow yourself to relax a little bit, and let the Master work out His plan. He got this!

Purpose Prayer for Today

Father God, thank You! Thank You for the blueprint, the plan You have for my life. Thank You that I no longer have to try to figure it all out. I just have to let You be You, and I have to trust You. Help me release control over the things I can't control. Help me not to worry about *how* my dreams, desires, and goals will come to pass. But help me remember *by whom* my dreams, desires, and goals will come to pass. I declare I will not get anxious and discouraged because the blueprint is already written. Instead, I will posture myself in prayer and position myself in action to fulfill the purpose You have for me. In Jesus's name, Amen.

Day 2

Are you a person who must control everything, or do you tend to let things flow? How has either of those mindsets helped or harmed you? Now that you know you don't have to have it all figured out, how does that help you move forward? In what ways can you demonstrate that you trust God's plan for your life?

_____

_____

_____

_____

_____

_____

_____

_____

_____

_____

_____

_____

Daily Affirmation: I am walking in peace, not panic, because I trust the plan God has for my life.

Day 3 Prayer

To everything there is a season, and a time for every purpose under heaven. —Ecclesiastes 3:1 KJV

What Is Purpose?

The simplest answer to that most universally asked question is this. Purpose is the reason why something exists or the reason something was created. Purpose is the solution to a problem. Take the airplane for example. Before the Wright Brothers created the first successful airplane, travel was complicated. Many years ago, it took a long time for people to travel short distances. The brothers decided to create a product that would solve that problem. First, they laid the blueprint, and then they began to build. The airplane was created to solve the problems of travel. Even though there were failed attempts, it was only a matter of time before they succeeded.

God created everything, including you, for a purpose. This means God created you with a gift that solves a problem for mankind. Gifts come in numerous ways, shapes, and forms. Your job is to acknowledge and accept that you have something we all need. Like the Wright Brothers, discovering what that is may be a process of failed attempts and through trial and error. However, as long as you keep building, it is truly only a matter of time before you will succeed. Don't stop pursuing your purpose. Keep building!

Purpose Prayer for Today

Father God, thank You that there is a time and a season for me to walk in my purpose. Thank You that You chose to create me at such a time as this. Thank You that, in this season of my life, my purpose will be made clear. Before the airplane ever took off in the air, the Wright brothers placed everything it needed on the inside of it. The engine, the gauges, and the cockpit, were all built into the plane first. Help me to remember that everything I need to fulfill my purpose is also built on the inside of me. I declare today I will not give up at failed attempts. I will not retreat to my comfort zone when things get uncomfortable. I have what it takes, and I will live out my purpose! In Jesus's Name, Amen.

Day 3

What universal issues do you feel strongly about? What world problems do you feel born to solve? How can you use your story and experiences to help solve that problem? Now that you know God placed everything you need inside you to fulfill your purpose, what are your next steps?

_____
_____
_____
_____
_____
_____
_____
_____
_____
_____
_____
_____
_____

Daily Affirmation: I am here on Earth to solve a problem. I have something that someone needs.

Day 4 Prayer

A man's gift makes room for him and brings him before great men. —Proverbs 18:16, NKJV

You Have a Gift!

Do you remember how you felt on Christmas Eve when you were a kid? The anticipation of opening your gifts was so heavy you could hardly sleep! As a mom now, I love to see the anticipation and impatience of my boys. They're constantly asking me questions and hinting about what they want. My oldest even sneaks around our house looking for where his gifts may be hidden.

I wonder what happens to that excitement and anticipation when we become adults. What is it about life that makes us lose our childlike enthusiasm about our God-given gifts? Could it be that we don't even know we have gifts? Maybe you lack excitement or maybe you lack interest because you lack awareness. Many of us don't even realize what we are packing.

Friend, let me tell you something. When you came to this earth, you came fully loaded. Every person God created came with specific power-packing gifts. The late great Myles Munroe said it best: "God hid your future in a place He knew you couldn't miss—inside of you!"

Like my older son, you have to search for the hidden things of God. He has already given you a clue; *it's hidden within.* This devotional is a jump-start for your faith, but it's definitely not the end goal. Get in the Word, stay in prayer, and go looking around His house for your gifts. I can only imagine what you are really working with. It's time to get to work and start unwrapping those gifts; someone is waiting on you!

Purpose Prayer for Today

Most gracious Heavenly Father, thank You for reminding me I am gifted. Thank You that even if I haven't fully used my gifts or if I have misused my gifts, they still belong to me. Thank You that what You have given to me, no person, not even me, can take away. Father, I am asking You to show me what's hidden on the inside of me. Allow me to not only recognize my gifts, but to refine and define them so I can reach my full potential. I declare today that my gifts will open doors for me that no man can shut. My gifts will put me in the presence of people with the power to bless me. From this day forward, I commit to unwrapping every gift hidden under Heaven for me. In Jesus's name, Amen.

Day 4

What are some of your natural gifts? What do people usually come to you for? Are there any gifts, abilities, or skills you've overlooked or dismissed? How can use your gifts to serve others and glorify God?

_____
_____
_____
_____
_____
_____
_____
_____
_____
_____
_____
_____

Daily Affirmation: I am fully loaded with God-given gifts that will make a difference in the lives of others.

Day 5 Prayer

Being confident of this very thing, that He who has begun a good work in you will complete it until the day of Jesus Christ. —Philippians 1:6, NKJV

It's Just the Beginning!

My all-time favorite sport is football. I schedule my whole life around the Ohio State Buckeyes during football season. But I have this love-hate thing about my Buckeyes when it comes to how they start. More times than not, they start off slow. It seems like it takes them time to gain momentum. The first half or so, it's like they're warming up. Neither the coaches nor the team ever seem to panic though. They just keep showing up and running the plays.

Although I don't like the slow the start because I don't enjoy being on pins and needles, I love their confidence. The coach doesn't panic, so the team doesn't panic. The coach is confident in what they have practiced. He is confident that, as long as they do on the field what they trained for off the field, they will finish with the win.

Sister-friend, can you see where I'm going with this?

You may feel like you have a slow start. You may feel like you aren't where you should be. You may not like being on pins and needles. Maybe you don't like not knowing the end result. You may feel like this game called life has started but you haven't gained any momentum in your first half.

But listen, your coach, who is called Christ, is confident in the work He has begun in you. And if He is confident, then you need to be like the Buckeyes and cease from panicking. God is not finished with you. God is not calling time-outs every time you fumble. God is saying, "Just run the play, babe." In the end, you *will* get the win.

Here's the catch though. *How are you going to run the play if you aren't reading His playbook*? You can't expect to know what to do if you haven't trained off the field. We all fall guilty of wanting the win without putting in the work, but to win the game, you have to know how to play it. Commit to studying the Book and practice the plays by exercising your faith. This is just the beginning, girl. You haven't seen nothing yet!

Purpose Prayer for Today

Hallelujah to the Most High! Father, thank You for the confidence You have in me even when I am not confident in myself. Thank You that You are a God who doesn't panic or lose Your cool when I drop the ball. Thank You that this is just my beginning and You will finish everything You started in me. I ask that You help me with Your playbook. Show me how to run these plays so I can get my win. Give me understanding and clarity. I am claiming my end will be better than my beginning. I am gaining my momentum. I will not panic because now I know the plays for my purpose are connected to Your Book. *I am a winner*, and it is so. In Jesus's name, Amen.

Day 5

Do you ever feel like you've had a slow start with your purpose or with your life? How can you use your off seasons to prepare for game time? Now that you know the key to winning the game is reading God's Book, what commitments are you willing to make to get more familiar with it?

_____

_____

_____

_____

_____

_____

_____

_____

_____

_____

Daily Affirmation: I am on the winning team. I am more than a conqueror, and my end will be better than my beginning.

Day 6 Prayer

Commit to the Lord whatever you do, and he will establish your plans. —Proverbs 16:3, NIV

I Mean, It's Whatever

Have you ever heard or used the term "it's whatever" in conversation? It's sort of a universal slang that means something doesn't matter or it's no biggie, nothing major or important. If I could assign an image to that phrase, it would be someone shrugging their shoulders. My son's friends will come over and ask him if he wants to either play basketball or walk to the store, and he usually responds, "I mean, it's whatever." Then, they decide what to do and go do it.

This phrase, "I mean, it's whatever," reminds me of the demeanor of our majestic and sovereign Holy God. As magnificent and wonderful as He is, Scripture proves to me that God looks down from His throne and shrugs His shoulders and says, "It's whatever, daughter."

Don't believe me? Let me prove it to you.

- The people of Israel were being chased by the Egyptian army. They got to the Red Sea and God looked and said, "It's whatever," no biggie. Bam! He split the Red Sea, and His people crossed over. (Exodus 14)

- There was a group of hungry people in Galilee, five thousand people to be exact. Jesus wanted to feed them, but there was only a little boy with two fish and five loaves of bread. Jesus looked and said, "It's whatever." He blessed the bread, and all the people ate with more than enough left over. (John 6)

- Still not convinced? Over two thousand years ago, a disciple named Judas (influenced by Satan) thought he was getting over by betraying Jesus. Jesus took all those beatings and accusations and afterwards lifted His hands and said, "It's whatever," and He laid down His life that *you* might live. (Matthew 26 & 27)

Although He did not technically say "it's whatever" His actions plus scripture prove to us that God is more easygoing than we think. Whatever you want to do, He is saying, "Make a plan for it and commit it to Me."

You want to be a homeowner—it's whatever. You want to start a business—it's whatever. You want a new car—it's whatever. You want to start that nonprofit—it's whatever. You want to be debt free—it's whatever.

Friend, there is nothing too big, too small, or too hard for God. Whatever you do or plan to do, do with a good heart. Do it with pure motives. The key is to have a plan He can establish. However, having a plan also requires action. You don't get to shrug your shoulders and say "it's whatever." Only our Father can do that. But you do get to make your plan, give it to Him, and let Him work out the details. Start thinking about the things you want and plan for them. Even if it's a small plan, that's okay. God can do much with little!

Purpose Prayer for Today

Father God, thank You that nothing is too hard for You. Thank You that no one or nothing can stop Your plans from being established. Thank You that although You sit high, You are more down-to-Earth than we realize. When I tell You my biggest dreams, You say, "That's cool. It's whatever. I will do it for you." God, help me not to be timid with my prayers to You. Help me to ask big and think big. Help me to give You something to work with by devising a plan and taking action. I declare today I will not get caught up in the details. I will do exactly what the Word says. I will commit *whatever* I do to You, and You will see to it that it gets done. In Jesus's name, Amen.

Day 6

Everyone has plans, but not everyone commits those plans to the Lord. Are there any plans you have made without committing them to the Lord? What are your plans for your life? How do you want to be remembered? What type of legacy do you want to live and leave? Write out your plans and commit them to God.

_____
_____
_____
_____
_____
_____
_____
_____
_____
_____
_____
_____

Daily Affirmation: I am committing my plans to God, and therefore, I know they will succeed.

Day 7 Prayer

And on the seventh day God ended His work which He had done, and He rested on the seventh day from all His work which He had done. —Genesis 2:2, NKJV

Resting Is a Part of Working

Hey, you, purpose chaser. Go-getter. Hustler. Hard worker. Multiprenuer. Mom-of-all-trades. I have a message from God for you. Get some rest!

In the midst of pursuing your purpose, in the midst of building an empire, in the midst of slaying goals, and working three jobs, please take care of yourself and rest. I found it fitting to choose this scripture for day 7 of our challenge because *while our faith requires action, our bodies require rest.*

Have you ever thought about why God rested on the seventh day? I mean He is God. All He had to do was say "Let there be," and it was. He didn't hit the ground running. He didn't hire a bunch of brick-laying angels to lay the foundation of the world. He sat on His throne, and *He spoke* everything into existence. I believe God, being the great father that He is, rested so He could be an example for us. There is certainly a time to work, but there is also a time to rest. He wanted to show us that even though He is God, He chose to incorporate rest in His work. He intended for rest to be such an imperative part of our routine that our bodies will begin to shut down and rebel against us when we deny them rest. On the days when I am really tired, or if I've had a series of restless nights, my attitude is not really nice. I'm irritable, I have a headache, I can't think clearly, and for some odd reason, I eat like crap.

Resting in God is not only sleeping, but also quiet time to yourself and quiet time with God. It's getting a book and going to your secluded place. It's listening to inspiring sermons or podcasts that feed your spirit. It's taking a day off work while the kids are at school just to do nothing. It's sleeping in. It's sneaking to get your favorite ice cream and eating it in the car so you can enjoy it alone (chocolate chip cookie dough for me).

God's voice is so much clearer when you're rested. The spiritual downloads are so much more potent when you're rested. How can you pursue your purpose if you are tired, irritable, and unable to think clearly? Sis, whatever rest looks like for you, listen to your body, and do it. Rest is a part of your work!

Purpose Prayer for Today

Most gracious Heavenly Father, thank You for rest. Thank You that I have the clearance to do nothing on some days. Thank You for setting the example and showing me that *rest is not an option; it is a requirement*. Help me not to feel bad or unproductive when I stop on purpose. Show me what productive rest looks like for me. Help me not to feel bad when I treat myself because I am worthy and I deserve a break. I deserve to reward myself.

I come against the spirit of guilt and shame. I come against the mindset that says work, work, and work. I rebuke the spirit of busyness. I decree and declare that I will rest consistently. I will take time to regularly renew my mind, body, and spirit. In Jesus's name, Amen.

Day 7

Are you getting enough rest? What does rest look like for you? How will you incorporate rest in your life? Now that you know resting is a part of working, are you committed to consistent rest?

_____
_____
_____
_____
_____
_____
_____
_____
_____
_____
_____
_____

Daily Affirmation: I am worthy of good rest. I will be intentional about giving my mind, body, and spirit the rest they need.

Day 8 Prayer

Be still and know that I am God. —Psalm 46:10, NKJV

This May Hurt a Little

In addition to getting rest, we need to learn to be still. Being still and knowing is quite different from resting. Let me give you an example. Take a moment and imagine yourself at the doctor's office for your annual flu shot. The doctor ties that little band around your arm in order to insert the needle. You flinch a little, but you brace yourself and sit *still* because you *know* that although it's going to hurt a little, it's something you need. You trust that the doctor is inflicting momentary pain for a greater gain, which is your health.

This is what I believe God means when He says to be still and know. Although some things we go through in life are painful, causing us to flinch and even cry, *the momentary pain is for an eternal gain.* Being still means although it may hurt, although you may not understand it, you *trust* your Heavenly Doctor has your best interest at heart. It means you *know* it's all working together for the good even when you don't know what that looks like.

When you get a flu shot, you can never be sure if you would have caught the flu without it. But you get the shot just to be on the safe side. Being still and knowing is the same. You choose to trust God even when you can't trace Him. When you trust God, you are always being on the safe side.

When it comes to pursuing your God-given purpose, don't forget to be still and know. God is not going to tell you His plans A to Z for your life. He's going to give you a few doses at a time. Try not get anxious or worried or think too far ahead. You don't have to rush anything or anyone; just be still and know.

Purpose Prayer for Today

Father God, thank You that You have it all under control and I don't have to figure everything out. Thank You that although some things You allow in my life hurt, they're still for my health, my good, my future, and for Your plan. Lord, show me how to be still when I begin to squirm too much. Help me to trust You when I can't trace You. Today, I choose to be still. I choose to trust the process. I am going to be on the safe side and know You are God. My times are in Your hands, and I know everything You have for me is all good. In Jesus's name, Amen.

Day 8

Do you ever find yourself getting anxious, worried, and antsy about something? What events can you recall that caused momentary pain for a greater gain? Are you are currently worried about anything? Now that you understand God has your best interest in mind in all circumstances, how can you be still and trust in Him?

_____
_____
_____
_____
_____
_____
_____
_____
_____

Daily Affirmation: I am being still and trusting God to work everything out for my good. I am not worried or stressed.

Day 9 Prayer

And Saul also went home to Gibeah; and valiant men went with him, whose hearts God had touched. But some rebels said, "How can this man save us?" So they despised him, and brought him no presents. But he held his peace.
—1 Samuel 10:26-27 NKJV

Look Out for Haters

You are on day 9, and you've been praying about all the good things God has in store for you. However, I would do you an injustice to make you think that while you pursue your purpose everyone is going to root you on. Here's some context behind today's scripture.

Saul had just been chosen as king of Israel, and many people celebrated him when he was anointed as king. Verse 26 tells us many valiant men went with Saul. In other words, these men were brave, heroic, and mighty, and God had touched their hearts to follow and support Saul. But verse 27 tells us there were also some rebels, who, in today's terms, were haters. They whispered amongst each other, "How can this man, this nobody, this regular guy, be our king?" Their refusal to bring the king gifts (which was the custom back then) exposed their envy.

As you step out on faith, as you walk in your purpose, you will encounter two types of people. There will be those who are assigned to you, those family members, friends, and strangers who support you and who are happy for you. There are the people whose hearts God has touched for you. But you will also encounter haters. You will encounter people who smile in your face but really despise your gifts. As my former mentor once said, they will be "annoyed by your anointing." Some will do a good job concealing it, but others will expose their envy. They will drift away. They will try to kill your dream and destroy your seed before it even takes root. They may show up as if they support you, but something will be off. They won't support your cause, and they may even criticize you. Even when you can't see it, you can sense the envy. Your spirit, your intuition, will tell you something has changed. Pay attention to that feeling.

You may be surprised by who has changed or jumped ship, but don't dismiss it. It can be disheartening, but you can't let that stop you. Be like Saul and hold your peace. Saul was well aware of his haters, but he didn't yell, "Off with their heads!" No, he held his peace. He didn't say a word.

Sis, I encourage you to do the same. *When someone shows you who they are, believe it—but hold your peace.* Don't get caught up in arguments and useless disputes. Understand there will always be haters and their number one job is to kill what God has birthed in you. Keep your distance, love from a distance, but keep pushing your purpose. Besides, if God be for you, who can be against you?

Purpose Prayer for Today

Dear Heavenly Father, thank You for the people assigned to me. Thank You for those whose hearts You have touched for the cause you put in me. Thank You for the anointing You have over me. Lord, help me to hold my peace when people begin to hate, especially when those haters are friends, family members, and people I expected to cheer me on. Guard my heart against disappointment and anger. Give me the strength to recognize them but to hold my peace and to keep walking in my calling. I ask You to expose those who secretly envy me and don't mean well by me. Remove anyone from my circle who no longer fits. I decree and declare I will be surrounded by those whose hearts You have touched. I will walk in wisdom, discernment, and peace. I will not be moved, and no one can stop what You have started in me. In Jesus's name, Amen.

Day 9

Have you ever experienced a loved one, friend, or stranger inwardly or outwardly hating on you? Have you ever sensed or discerned the spirit of jealousy around you? How have you handled those situations? Now you know that God will send people who are for you as you pursue your purpose. You also know that no one can stop His plans for you. So how will you handle an encounter with a jealous or envious person?

_____
_____
_____
_____
_____
_____
_____
_____
_____
_____

Daily Affirmation: I am standing on solid ground. I will not be bothered or moved when I encounter a hating spirit.

Day 10 Prayer

"Yet you have not because you ask not." —James 4:2
NKJV

What Are You Asking For?

I have four beautiful goddaughters who I love dearly. If I had the power to give them the world, I would. One Christmas, they all asked for different gifts, so I got them each what they wanted. One of my goddaughters wanted a camera, and another wanted some artistic items. When they opened their gifts, my artistic goddaughter looked at her mom with disappointment and said, "Mom, I wanted one of those cameras too." And I said "Goddaughter, I asked you what you wanted, and you said you wanted art supplies. If you would've told me you wanted the camera, I would've gotten it for you!"

Like my goddaughter, many of us look at another person's gift and blame our Father for not giving us the same. We compare ourselves to others on social media. We compare their number of followers and number of likes to ours. Or we compare ourselves to our coworkers, friends, and even family members. We feel less than or intimidated by someone else's gift, as if we don't measure up. We no longer want our gifts because we want what they have.

God's response to us is similar to my response to my goddaughter. He is saying "Child of mine, ask me for what you want, and

I will give it to you!" But here's the key. Verse 3 of that scripture says "When you ask, you do not receive, because you ask with wrong motives, that you may spend what you get on your pleasures." Do you remember the prayer for day 6? It talked about committing our plans to Him with pure motives and good intentions, and when we do, then it's whatever.

When you ask God for what you want, ask yourself why you want it. Why do you want that business? Why do you want that house or property? Why do you want a promotion? Why do you want more followers or clients? Why do you want to quit your job? Why do you want a husband? Is it for your own gain, your own selfish desires, or to be a blessing to someone else? Is it for God's glory to be revealed? Is it to look important in the eyes of God or in the eyes of man?

If you haven't already, just ask, "God, what is my purpose? What are my gifts?" Then assess yourself. Make sure you know your why behind every question you ask. God is waiting on you to just ask!

Purpose Prayer for Today

Dear Gracious and Heavenly Father, thank You that You are willing to give me whatever I ask for. Thank You for being a generous God, a God who not only can give me the world but wants to! I must admit I haven't always asked for things with pure motives, and I apologize. I understand that while some prayers will be answered at the right time, other prayers have not been answered because my *why* was wrong. I ask that You search my heart and help me to understand why I want the things I ask for. Help me to ask You for things with the right intent. I know I deserve the things I desire; just help me to be clear on what to ask for. There are also some things You are just waiting for me to be bold enough to ask You for. So today I declare I won't be too scared to ask You for anything. I understand Your answer may be yes, no, or wait, but I will not cheat myself by not at least asking. I will not walk around wishing. I will open my mouth, ask You, and trust Your timing. In Jesus's name, Amen.

Day 10

Are there things you have wanted but haven't actually asked for? What expectations have you had of both people and God that you haven't clearly shared? Write down the things you are asking God for, and then write down why you are asking God for each of those things.

_____
_____
_____
_____
_____
_____
_____
_____
_____
_____
_____
_____
_____

Daily Affirmation: I am clear on the things I want out of life. My motives are pure, and I deserve the things I desire.

Day 11 Prayer

But when you ask, you must believe and not doubt, because the one who doubts is like a wave of the sea, blown and tossed by the wind. —James 1:6 NIV

Ride the Waves

We just admitted yesterday that we have not because we ask not. Now here is another one of those disclaimers God so often attaches to His promises. When you ask, you must believe and you can't doubt. That is easier said than done though, right? We are humans, talking to an invisible God and asking for things we know we can't achieve by ourselves, and now we are commanded not to doubt!

Have your kids, spouse, or a family member ever came in the house and said, "I'm sooo hungry"? Even worse, do they moan and groan and complain about how they're starving *while* you are actively preparing their meal? Or think about when the kids repeatedly ask you to buy something when you're just waiting for payday to make the purchase. After constant complaining and pleading, you finally respond, "If you ask me *one more time*, you ain't getting it!"

Well, beloved, how do you think God feels when you ask Him for something and then complain and plead like you aren't going to receive it?

When your kids see you preparing dinner but continue to complain about how hungry they are, as if you don't feed them, it is irritating and offensive. When your kids see you working hard every day but act as if they don't have enough, they seem ungrateful. When people doubt you and don't take your word at face value, you get offended. Well, God is the same way. He too could eventually say, "Daughter, if you are going to keep complaining and crying like I don't feed you and take care of you, *you ain't getting it!*"

Repeatedly asking in disbelief demonstrates a lack of faith. Like the waves of the sea you have rising hope followed by sinking doubt. When the waves of life are high, you feel good, but when things get low, you worry and doubt. God will not move in that. You must remain steady and ride the waves with faith and hope at all times.

God is already preparing a way and an answer for you. You've asked Him to reveal your purpose. You've asked for the things you desire. So now, thank Him in advance. That's faith at its finest. Imagine how you would feel if before you even made their plates, your loved ones said, "Thanks for a great meal. I know this meal is about to be so good. You are the best mom/wife/cook ever!" Wouldn't that make you want to do more? The same goes for God when you give thanks *before* He has even finished preparing what you've asked for, before payday even comes, He will bless you even more!

Purpose Prayer for Today

Lord, thank You that You have already prepared a table for me. Thank You that You are much more patient with me than I am with my loved ones. Thank You that You are not easily irritated or offended because Your word says You are slow to anger and full of mercy. Teach me how to ride the waves of life with faith, hope, and confidence. Help me not to doubt, not to worry, and not to stress over the things I have asked You for. God, I am believing You for a lot of things, and although I may get nervous from time to time, I will make my best effort not to complain and doubt as of today. Instead, I am going to make a list of everything I have asked You for, everything I am believing You for. Then I am going to thank You in advance for each of those things, one by one, and expect You to do even more! In Jesus's name, Amen.

Day 11

Have people ever doubted your word and your promises? How did that make you feel? Have you ever prayed about things and then worried or complained about those things? Now that you know doubt and unbelief cannot accompany a prayer, what adjustments will you make? Go back to the list you made yesterday, and thank God in advance for the things you are asking Him for.

_____
_____
_____
_____
_____
_____
_____
_____
_____
_____

Daily Affirmation: I am full of faith and confidence in God. I am believing Him to answer my prayers, and I thank Him in advance.

Day 12 Prayer

But they that wait upon the Lord shall renew their strength; they shall mount up with wings as eagles; they shall run, and not be weary; and they shall walk and not faint. —Isaiah 40:31 KJV

Wait for It

Do you mind waiting for things, or do you prefer to get them when you ask for them? Personally, I prefer getting things right away. However, by now we know our God is super patient, and He is never in a hurry. This means we are going to have to wait sometimes. Isaiah tells us that as we wait, our strength is being renewed.

Many of us have been waiting a long time for a particular person or thing. Some of us are waiting for situations and circumstances to change. It's been so long since you asked for a child, a husband, a job, or whatever you requested. It's been so long that you've prayed for that loved one to come to Christ or for that child to get on track, but it seems like they get worse. No matter what, all humans have one thing in common. We are waiting for something. Sometimes, while we wait, our faith grows weak. We lose hope, we lose enthusiasm, and we get to a point where we tell ourselves we don't even care anymore. We get that "it is what it is" attitude.

But the Bible tells us that when you wait on God, four things will happen:

1. **You renew your strength.** This isn't the "lifting weight" kind of strength, but the strength of recognizing your weakness. It takes a strong person to admit they're weak, tired, and hopeless. Being vulnerable is a sign of strength. When you confess to God your weakness, it gives you strength because you acknowledge He is God, and you are but a mere person. You release the responsibility of trying to make things happen and choose to relax and trust Him. The Bible says God gives power to the weak; to those who have no might, He increases strength (Isaiah 29 KJV). God also says that His strength is made perfect in our weakness.

2. **You mount up with wings as eagles.** What's the significance of eagle wings? Why not owl wings or vulture wings? Eagles are considered chiefs over all winged creatures. They are the dominant birds of the sky. No creature can soar as high as the eagle. Eagles symbolize power, and the presence of the eagle bestows freedom and courage to look ahead.

3. **You will run and not be weary.** As adults we don't have the same stamina we had when we were kids. We grow tired and winded after running for a long time. But actively waiting and trusting on God allows us to keep moving forward without growing weary and throwing in the towel.

4. **You will walk and not faint.** As we grow tired running, we can also grow faint walking. Walking with God isn't always easy. Walking in faith can be hard. Even in the natural, walking for a long time could cause us to faint. But as long we walk with our gaze fixed on Christ, we will not misstep or faint.

So be encouraged today. I know you are tired of waiting. I know your faith is weak in some places. Better yet, God knows, and He is saying, "Wait for me, daughter. Like my eagle, you are about to soar!"

Purpose Prayer for Today

Dear God, thank You that when I am weak You are strong. Thank You for not expecting me to have it all together all the time. Thank You for understanding I am just a person and I need moments of renewed strength and hope. Lord, help me to be vulnerable with You. Help me to recognize and admit when I am weak and need Your strength. Help me to wait on You with the right mindset and attitude, with hope, with trust and expectation. Today I am professing every area of weakness to You. I am admitting to You where I have lost hope. I will lay every one of my burdens at Your feet, and I will lift my hands to You in praise. I expect that, with hands lifted, my wings are being developed, and like your eagle, I'm going to *soar* over everything that ever had me down. In Jesus's name, Amen.

Day 12

What have you been waiting on God for? Have you grown weary in the waiting? In what areas do you need to be vulnerable and transparent with God? How has the promise of this scripture empowered you to wait with expectation?

_____
_____
_____
_____
_____
_____
_____
_____
_____
_____
_____
_____

Daily Affirmation: I am waiting on God with expectation. My strength is renewed today, and I will not faint.

Day 13 Prayer

Immediately the father of the child cried out with tears, "Lord, I believe; help my unbelief!" —Mark 9:24, NKJV

Umm, Lord, I Don't Know

I'm confident that by now a purpose chord has been struck in you. You may not be clear or fully convinced, but I know those wheels are turning in the direction of purpose! And today I want to let you know it's okay if you don't know it all yet. It's okay if you believe some of the things you have been reading while others have been hard to receive.

The person who spoke in Mark 9:24 was a father, and his son had a serious issue. Today, we would call it a severe mental illness, but the Bible called it a mute spirit. This father wanted to believe his son could be healed. He heard everyone talking about this Jesus, who healed and did all these miracles, but he still wasn't one hundred percent sure. So when he had the opportunity to talk to Jesus, he basically said "I believe some parts of what I've heard about You. I know there's something real about You, but another part of me is having a hard time believing You are who You say are. I have a hard time believing You would do this for me."

Jesus didn't say, "Dude, you mean to tell me after all the miracles I have done, after all you you've heard, you don't believe Me?"

He didn't rebuke the father and send him away. Guess what He did. He said, "All things are possible if you can believe," and He healed the son immediately!

This word is for you if you feel like this father. Maybe for the most part you believe you have a gift and a purpose in life. Maybe you see how other people have been blessed and how their dreams came true, so you know it's possible. But you ask, "Is it possible for me? Will He really do for me what He has done for others? Will I really be successful? Do I really have something to offer the world? Am I really gifted at something? Will I really get the things I've been asking Him for?"

I want you to know God isn't offended or mad when you ask these questions. As a matter of fact, I believe God likes it when we are in these moments of unbelief because it gives Him room to prove Himself. I shared how we have to believe and not doubt, but I want to reassure you that everything is a process and God knows that. Don't beat yourself up if you are not fully convinced about God, your purpose, or some areas of your life. Just be vulnerable and express your doubts to God. *Not being sure, not knowing, or not believing won't take your gift or your purpose away.* Those are yours to keep. Your doubts won't cause you to forfeit your dreams. When you confess that you have unbelief in some areas, God's response will be like it was to the father in this scripture. He will prove it to you!

Purpose Prayer for Today

Lord God, thank You that You are not mad at some of my areas of disbelief. Thank You for Your desire to prove Yourself to me.

Help me to be vulnerable and admit to You my areas of unbelief, and help me understand why I feel that way. I know You have created me for a purpose. Help me to see myself the way You see me—beautiful, strong, and well deserving of *all* Your blessings. Help me accept the fact that all things are possible for me when I believe in You. If You have done it for others, why wouldn't You do it for me? Today I declare that even when I have moments of unbelief, I will push toward my purpose. I won't let it stop me from going after what You have for me. Your thoughts toward me are good, and I will not accept anything less than that. In Jesus's name, Amen.

Day 13

What areas of unbelief are you struggling with? Confess them to God. What quiets your doubts and elevates your confidence in Christ? Compare how you see yourself to how God sees you. Do they line up? How can you leverage what you know against the things you don't know?

_____

_____

_____

_____

_____

_____

_____

_____

_____

_____

_____

_____

Daily Affirmation: I am a believer. I am replacing every area of unbelief with the Word of God.

Day 14 Prayer

There are diversities of gifts, but the same Spirit. There are differences of ministries, but the same Lord. And there are diversities of activities, but it is the same God who works all in all. But the manifestation of the Spirit is given to each one for the profit of all. —1 Corinthians 12:4-7, NKJV

One Size Doesn't Fit All

Have you ever tried to shop for clothes online, but instead of providing different options with a size chart, the website said one size fits all? If you're anything like me, you hesitated to buy it because you didn't want to run the risk that it wouldn't fit.

Today's passage shows you when it comes to your purpose and your gifts, one size does not fit all. The Word says we all have different gifts, are called to different ministries, and are called to do different activities. But it also says all these differences come from *the same God* for the profit of all.

In general conversation, I've noticed some people minimize their gifts or their calling because it doesn't look like another person's gift or calling. They feel like since someone else has already started a blog, launched a podcast, or written a book, they would look like copy cats if they did the same. At the other end of the spectrum, people refuse to share their ideas and inventions because they fear being copied. Other people don't want to expose their gifting for fear another person will be intimidated or offended.

Sis, I can tell you that when it comes to the kingdom closet, one size does not fit all! We all fall guilty of worrying about what others will think. But let today's scripture marinate for a minute. *God has a specific assignment only for you and for you to reach a specific group of people.* There are over seven billion people in the world, which means there are seven billion ways to do something. Sis, please don't let the fear of not "fitting in" stop you from pursuing your purpose. If you go to the bread aisle at Walmart, you'll notice Sara Lee didn't stop selling her brand of bread because Walmart created a Great Value brand. To each their own! There's a group of people who prefer Sara Lee, and there are people who prefer Great Value, but either way, *they are getting fed!*

I challenge you to unapologetically explore your gifts and walk in them. People are hungry for your brand! It doesn't matter who is doing this or that when it's all *from* God *for* His Kingdom. Sis, feed the people with your gifts, and not only will they profit but you will too. There is no gift too big or small, too common or too average. Once you discover what He wants you to do and do it, you'll find nothing or no one can even compare!

Purpose Prayer for Today

Lord God, thank You that what You have for me is for me. Thank You that there is a particular group of people waiting for what I have to offer. Thank you that we don't live in a world where everyone and everything is the same. How boring would that be anyway? Thank You that I can be authentically me and fit in where I'm supposed to be. Help me to release the mindset that my calling isn't good enough. Help me to gladly accept what You have called me to do. Help me to figure out who I am and do it on purpose. I declare today I will not minimize, ignore, or compare my gifts. I am going to lace my shoes up and run in my own lane. In Jesus's name, Amen.

Day 14

How can you take ownership of the things God has placed inside you? In what ways have you compared your gifting to others? How has that limited or stopped you from moving forward? What steps are you going to take to pursue the path of purpose God has for you?

_____
_____
_____
_____
_____
_____
_____
_____
_____
_____

Daily Affirmation: I am intentionally set apart by God to do what He has called me do. I am at my best when I am my authentic self.

Day 15 Prayer

I have fought the good fight, I have finished the race, I have kept the faith. —2 Timothy 4:7, NKJV

Don't Stop! Run Your Race!

You are halfway through this devotional, and I pray it has been a blessing to you. I am so proud that you've made it this far. I want to encourage you today to keep going. Not only do I want you to stay committed to the devotions and the journaling, but I want you to keep searching, keep trying, keep building, and keep pursuing purpose!

While I thought about putting today's verse at the end of this book, the Holy Spirit led me to put it smack dab in the middle. Why? Because I believe the middle is where many of us get stuck. At the beginning, we start off strong, and by the end, we have enough stamina to see the finish line and go for it. But the middle—well, the middle gets messy. We have all experienced some sort of messy middle. We all start off with stamina that wears off somewhere in the middle.

The middle is when you've been reading these devotionals and praying these prayers, and *nothing* has changed. The middle is right around 2:30 or 3:00 in the afternoon, when time slows down, and you're ready to clock out from your 9-to-5. The middle is when all you are trying to do is live right and pursue your purpose, and all hell breaks loose. The middle is when you gather the courage to write your first blog post or create your website, and your system crashes. The middle is when you've created a budget to pay off debt, and your car breaks down. The middle is when you had great plans for 2020, and COVID-19 hit.

Paul wrote today's scripture in a letter from prison. He had been through hell and high water, but he could confidently say he did *everything* God called him to do. He had been beaten, incarcerated, lied on, mocked, bitten by a poisonous snake—the list goes on. But in the midst of all that, he said *he fought a good fight, finished the race, and kept his faith*. Each of us has had some hard times. We've lost loved ones, lost a job, or run out of money. We've made mistakes. We were hurt, mistreated, taken advantage of, or cheated on. We all fall down, *but we get back up.*

Like Paul, I want you to get so determined that, as long you have breath in your body, you are going to finish the race. You won't stop fighting, you won't stop trying, you won't stop hoping, and you won't give up. You won't give up on your dreams, you won't give up on love, you won't give up on your kids or your spouse, and you won't give up on God. For every race and every competition, there is a reward, not for those who start well but for those who finish strong.

Finish strong my friend. Don't allow the enemy to keep you stuck in the middle. Don't let tests and trials trick you into believing God doesn't have anything for you. Don't get stagnant because you can't see results yet. *Keep running, keep running, keep running, and keep running!* Don't look behind you, sis. Look ahead. You only lose when choose to quit. The finish line is closer than you think. Ecclesiastes 9:11 (KJV) says, *The race is not given to the swift, nor the strong but he who endures until the end.*

Purpose Prayer for Today

Lord God, thank You that I have what it takes to finish my race. Thank You that this race I'm in is against no one but myself. Thank You that, as long as I keep running, I will do everything I was born to do. God, help me to stay the course through the middle. Help me not to give up, shy away, or retreat to my level of safety when things get thick. Help me to keep pushing until I birth every single thing in me. Give me a vision, a glimpse of what my end will look like, so I can keep going. Help me clear my mind and dust off the remnants of pain and confusion so I can pursue. I know the middle is designed to test my faith, to test my strength, and to reveal both who You are and who I am. I decree today that *I will finish strong. I will get the victory, and You will get the glory!* In Jesus's name, Amen.

Day 15

Are you experiencing any middle seasons in your life? How do you deal with setbacks and disappointments? Do you have the tendency to quit, or do you keep going? In what ways will you make sure you finish your race even when things get messy?

_____
_____
_____
_____
_____
_____
_____
_____
_____
_____
_____
_____
_____

Daily Affirmation: I am finishing the race God has set before me. I will not give up. I am finishing strong.

Day 16 Prayer

But thanks be to God, who gives us the victory through our Lord Jesus Christ. —1 Corinthian 15:57, NKJV

I Just Want to See You Win

I work out to a song by Derek Minor called "See You Win." He sings about how he wants to see everyone win and walk in the promises of God. I was reminded of that song at my son's basketball game one day. I thought about how the boys on the team didn't care who made the shots; they just wanted to win. Although they played different positions, they were all part of the same team, and their end goal was to see the team win.

Yesterday, we discussed running in your lane and finishing the race. Here's the second part to that. God not only wants you to finish your race; God wants to see you win! Finishing the race is good, but winning the race is better. Remember there are different ministries, gifts, and activities, but they all come from the same God. While we all have different positions, we are all on the same team. God has fixed the race for those of us who wear #teamJesus on our jersey. Today's word says God gives the people on His team the victory! Notice the word "gives." While you are staying in your lane and running your race, God is the one handing out trophies at the finish line. He is the one who says, "You win!"

When my son was younger, the sports league would let both teams win no matter the score. At the end of the game, every player was given a trophy. In the same way, God proclaims your victory, and to the next #teamJesus player, He says, "You win too! And you! And You!" With God, it doesn't matter your position. As long as you play, as long as you run on His team, you win. It doesn't matter who finishes before you or after you because we are all on the same team.

Sis, I want you to know it's not too late to win your race, but it's your race. No one can win it for you; no one can claim your trophy. Both your lane and your trophy have your name on them. Don't let the enemy trick you into thinking you are too young or too old to pursue purpose and win the race. That's a lie. As long as you have the ability to run, it's still your race. *The result you get lies in your decision to run or not.* God won't make you do anything. He will equip you with everything you need, and He will even fix it so you have won before you've even begun. It's up to you believe that and claim your trophy. So put your spiritual sneakers on, sis. Get to stretching, and get ready to run and claim what's yours!

Purpose Prayer for Today

Dear Lord, thank You that You have already *given* me the victory. Thank You that there is a trophy with my name on it, waiting to be claimed. Thank You for the reminder that I am only in a race against myself. I'm running toward everything You have just for me. Lord, I ask that You help me run my race. I refuse to be one of those people with unclaimed funds, unclaimed victories, and unclaimed gifts. Lord, I declare today I will claim everything that has my name on it. I won't let the fact that it may take some time to win discourage me. I won't allow my age to make me think it's not possible. Because your word says You will *give* me the victory, I will *take* it and hold my trophy high. In Jesus's name, Amen.

Day 16

Have you always seen yourself as a winner? How does it feel to know you were a winner before you even began? How will you ensure that you finish your race and receive your trophy? List at least five ways you can realign yourself when you begin to drift or get distracted from running in your lane.

_____
_____
_____
_____
_____
_____
_____
_____
_____
_____
_____
_____

Daily Affirmation: I am a winner. I am more than a conqueror. I have the victory in Jesus's name.

Day 17 Prayer

Then the Lord answered me and said: "Write the vision and make it plain on tablets, That he may run who reads it. For the vision is yet for an appointed time; But at the end it will speak, and it will not lie. Though it tarries, wait for it; Because it will surely come, It will not tarry."
—Habakkuk 2:2-3, NKJV

See It with Your Pen

Over the past two days, we've covered running and winning. Today, I want to give you another key to your success, which is writing your vision down on paper. I hosted my very first business event, a Vision Board Party, in December 2019. I chose this as the first event because I wanted everyone to know the importance of not only having a vision but writing it down and making it plain. Years ago, before my business She Pursues Purpose ever came to be, I wrote down in my journal "vision board party." In December 2019, it came to pass.

God told me to submit a piece of written content to a particular ministry in 2018. I didn't know how or when I was going to do it, but I wrote in my journal what I believed He told me to do. One day in the summer of 2019, my mentor contacted me and told me it had dropped in her spirit that I should do exactly what God had told me to do a year earlier. I sent a screenshot to her and showed her that I had written that down a year prior!

Thoughts are nothing more than thoughts, but the results come when you write them down and act on them. *When you know where you are going, you tend to move in that direction, consciously and subconsciously.*

Whether you realize it or not, God has given you visions for your future and visions for the promises He has made you. It can be easy to overlook, ignore, or simply forget what those are when you fail to write them down. For instance, do you ever write out a grocery list? Why do you do that? So you can go into the store with a clear understanding of what to buy. You won't waste time in the snack aisle if you plan to buy bananas. Do you ever write a to-do list for your day? If it says you have a doctor's appointment at 9:00 in the morning, then you know not to schedule anything else at that time and you don't forget the appointment.

"When you don't have a vision, distractions can look like opportunities." Writing down your vision will help direct your life. God has made me promises that haven't happened yet. I wrote them down and put them on my vision board so I can be on the lookout for them and intentionally move in their direction. I avoid wasting time and energy on things and people not aligned with my purpose. The Word tells us some parts of our vision are for an appointed time. Although it tarries (takes a while), it will still happen, so wait for it. Today I challenge you to put eyes on your ink pen.

Purpose Prayer for Today

Dear God, thank You for Your promises. Thank You for the power of writing things down. Thank You for Your divine ability to bring everything I write to pass. Lord, I am asking You for a fresh revelation. A fresh and clear vision for my life. Help me see the vision clearly so I can write it down clearly. Help me not to waste time and energy on people and things that are not aligned with the vision for my life. Help me remember that writing also includes waiting. Everything is not going to happen at once and on my timetable, but I trust You to bring it to life at the right time. Lord, I am going to write my vision, make it plain, and submit it to You. Thank You in advance for how You are going to not only bring it to pass but also exceed my expectations! In Jesus's name, Amen.

Day 17

Write down everything you see in your mind no matter how big, small, or impossible it may seem. Create sections in your journal for personal, family, and business. Write every vision you have for each section. Pray over your vision and trust God to align His universe and His people in a way that attracts and manifests every single thing you wrote.

_____

_____

_____

_____

_____

_____

_____

_____

_____

Daily Affirmation: I clearly see the vision for my life in every area of my life. Everything I write down will come to pass according to God's will and timing.

Day 18 Prayer

This man had been instructed in the way of the Lord; and being fervent in spirit, he spoke and taught accurately the things of the Lord, though he knew only the baptism of John. —Acts 18:25, NKJV

If Only You Knew

Today's scripture references a man named Apollos. Chapter 18 of Acts tells us Apollos was an eloquent man and mighty in the scriptures. He spoke and taught the Word of God in the synagogues. While there were many apostles and disciples teaching the Word during that time, Apollos was different. Why? Because, the Bible says, he *only* knew the baptism of John. Although, he wasn't scripted or versed in anything but the baptism, he took what he knew, and he worked it.

Now I want you to look within. Have you ever allowed what you didn't know to stop you from speaking and teaching what you did know? I will be the first to admit I've done this. I will even go a step further and admit that because of *who* I didn't know, I hesitated to do what I felt led to do.

I want you to know God already knows what you don't know. Yet, that has not stopped Him from wanting to use you. The enemy will use what you don't know against you if you're not careful. He will make you think the thing God is calling you to do or share isn't going to work because you don't know it all or don't know the right people. But God says, "Daughter, if you only knew the way I plan to enlarge your territory. If only you knew how I am going to take your little knowledge and experience and multiply them."

I want to challenge you to be like Apollos. Take what you have and work it to the best of your ability. Whatever experience, knowledge, or information you have, put all your effort and energy into growing mighty in that. Later in the same chapter, the Bible says a married couple, Aquila and Priscilla, took Apollos and taught him the Word of God more accurately. God sent people to Apollos who helped him grow in his calling and in his ministry. God did that because Apollos was willing to start with what he had and what he knew.

Friend, God plans to do the same for you. As you start where you are and work with what you have, God will send the right people and open the right doors for you. Make the decision today to take what you know and work it!

Purpose Prayer for Today

Father God, thank You for not holding the things I don't know against me. Thank You that You know all things and You are in control of my destiny. Father God, I am asking for the courage and clarity to take my knowledge and experiences and use them for Your glory. Help me to become a master of what I know. Help me to teach and help the people You have assigned to me with confidence. Lord, it doesn't matter what I know or who I know when You are my all-knowing and ever-present God. I release the fear, the worry, and the doubt, and I declare today I will work with what I have. As I work, I will expect You to send the right people and open the right doors for me. In Jesus's name, Amen.

Day 18

Have you ever doubted your calling or assignment because of what you didn't know or who you didn't know? What are some things you felt led to do, teach, or share that you decided not to do because of these reasons? What are you willing to do now that you've decided to work with what you have?

_____

_____

_____

_____

_____

_____

_____

_____

_____

_____

Daily Affirmation: I am working with what I have to bring God glory. I expect God will increase my territory and align me with the right relationships as I move forward.

Day 19 Prayer

Little by little I will drive them out from before you, until you have increased, and you inherit the land. —Exodus 23:30, NKJV

Crumb Fed

My husband and my boys love to eat snacks so much that I often feel buying them is a waste of money because as soon as I bring the snacks home, they eat them all at once. To prevent this, I leave out a few snacks and hide the rest so they can last longer. Recently, I left out an eighteen-pack of Lay's chips before I went to a workshop. When I came home, less than half the pack was left. My workshop was only from 3:00 to 6:00! I was so mad!

After my anger subsided, today's scripture came to mind. God had laid out many promises to His people in this chapter. He gave them instructions on how to obtain and maintain the blessings. He also gave them the terms under which they could forfeit those blessings. He promised to give them some land, but the land was currently inhabited by their enemies, so God told them He would drive their enemies out *little by little*. My little potato chip event at home helped me to understand why some blessings and promises can't come all at once and must come *little by little*.

What would have happened if God had driven out all their enemies in one day? What would have happened if God said, "Here you go, loads of empty land. You can figure it out from here," and just handed it over?

Naturally, we want everything God has for us right away. We want to be rich, we want to be homeowners, and we want to be business owners. We want all these things, but could we handle it all at once? *If God told you everything He was going to do for you, it would overwhelm you.* Nine times out of ten, it wouldn't excite you; it would scare you, and you wouldn't know what to do with it.

If God gave you a million bucks today, could you manage it? If God gave you a house today without giving you time to learn how to budget, save, and build your credit, could you maintain that blessing? Like my guys, many of us would eat all our snacks at once if God didn't crumb feed them to us.

God said He will give us things little by little until we increase. In other words, as we *increase in discipline, increase in self-control, increase in maturity, wisdom, strategy, obedience*, He will give us more. He does things a little at a time because of His tender mercies and lovingkindness. Being the humans we are, if our blessings came too quickly and too easily, we wouldn't appreciate them. We tend to appreciate the things we have to work for and fight for. How many times do we see on the news the loss or downfall of a young famous person who was afforded too much too soon?

Friend, God knows what He is doing. As *you* increase, your blessings will increase. The best way to increase is to stay in His word. He gives us everything we need to not only obtain the blessings but to also maintain them and inherit all He has for us. I offer many tools that will help you increase as your pursue. Join me at https://she-pursues-purpose.ck.page/newsletter to stay in the know! In the words of the late great Myles Munroe "God won't give you what you pray for. He gives you what you can manage."

Purpose Prayer for Today

Dear Father, thank You for Your wisdom. Thank You for knowing what I can manage and blessing me accordingly. Thank You that as I grow spiritually, mentally, and even physically, I will be able to handle more of what You have for me. Thank You for understanding that although I may want it all right now, it's better to receive it little by little. Lord, help me get to a place where I can receive more. Help me to be more disciplined in the areas where I lack discipline. Help me to grow in wisdom, obedience, self-control, and of course, in Your word. God, I declare that as I pursue my purpose and my promises, I will work on my areas of needed growth. I'd rather be in a position to obtain and maintain my blessings than to receive them and forfeit them. I *speak* increase over my life right now in Jesus's name, Amen.

Day 19

What do you need more of in your life? What areas do you need to increase in? What do you need less of in your life? Are there areas you need to manage better? If so, list those and write the steps you will take to improve.

_____
_____
_____
_____
_____
_____
_____
_____
_____
_____
_____
_____

Daily Affirmation: I am increasing in wisdom, discipline, strength, self-control, strategy, and obedience every day. My capacity to maintain my blessings is increasing today.

Day 20 Prayer

Dishonest money dwindles away, but whoever gathers little by little makes it grow. —Proverbs 13:11, NIV

Just a Little More

Yesterday's word immediately reminded me of the word for today. Yesterday we talked about the responsibility God has to give us our blessings little by little to ensure we can maintain them. Today, the responsibility of gathering little by little is on us so we can gain reasonably. There are so many scriptures throughout the Bible that talk about not being in a hurry to get rich. Not to love money. Not to exploit or take advantage of others to get rich. Proverbs 13:11 lets us know that dishonest money is fleeting; it won't last. But whoever works diligently, whoever works hard, and whoever saves, can expect their money to grow.

I've planned for my business, She Pursues Purpose, to be the way I retire from the corporate world. God has put this in my heart, and I know He is going to do it. I'm not sure when, but hear my declaration of faith friend: "I will walk in my purpose full time at the appointed time!" If your testimony is the same, shout amen! The key is that while I am in the corporate world, I am strategizing. I'm gathering little by little. I'm eliminating debt. I'm tithing and following the kingdom principles for money the best I know how! I am not in a hurry to get rich quick. I am working my job and letting my job work for me. I am funding my business. I am pursuing purpose not paper!

God is in no hurry to give us everything at once, but I want you to know God is not slack concerning His promises to you. He's teaching and preparing you, little by little, so you can be well rounded when the blessings overtake you. No matter what your current income is, there is more! But with that comes more responsibility and accountability. He wants to make sure He can trust you with more. God wants you to know that although you don't have everything you want, He will make sure you have everything you need. When you need a little more, He will give it to you.

My challenge for you is to keep gathering, little by little. Follow the kingdom principles for good success and wealth, and they will come to pass. As you *gather*, you are also *gaining* discipline, strategy, wisdom, knowledge, and self-restraint. God loves you, and He is bubbling with excitement to pour out such a blessing on you that you won't have room to store it! The key is to do it how He says first and then watch how He bless you with *more than enough*!

Purpose Prayer for Today

Heavenly Father, thank You for the blessings stored up for me and just waiting to be released. Thank You, Lord, that whether I make $600 a month or $6000 a month, *there is more for me*. Thank You for explaining in Your word how to gather, sow, and reap. I ask that you continue to teach me and show me how to manage my money in a way that brings You glory. Teach me in a way that proves to You I can be trusted with more. Help me to be disciplined with my finances wherever I may lack. Give me the right strategy for my situation so I can capitalize on my job, with my fixed income, or just with what I have. Today I declare I will gather, little by little, until it grows. I won't pursue money. I will pursue purpose because I know *my purpose will bring forth profit*. I receive all that is mine in Jesus's name. Amen.

Day 20

What's your relationship with money? Do you overspend, hoard, or spend and save reasonably? How can you leverage your current situation to work toward your future goals? What steps do you need to take to ensure your financial habits support your big picture?

_____

_____

_____

_____

_____

_____

_____

_____

_____

_____

Daily Affirmation: I obtain and maintain money wisely. I understand money is a means to push forth God's purpose, and therefore, I will gather, little by little, and gain strategy along the way.

Day 21 Prayer

And he said, "Thus says the Lord, 'Make this valley full of ditches ... You shall not see wind, nor shall you see rain; yet that valley shall be filled with water.' And this is a simple matter in the sight of the Lord. —2 Kings 3:16-18, NKJV

Prepare for the Promises

For the past two days we've discussed how our blessings and the process of discovering our purpose comes little by little. However, today's word helps us to get *prepared* for *sudden* overflow. The thing I know about God is that He loves to surprise us with blessings. He loves to send a random check in the mail, cancel a debt unexpectedly, or all of a sudden answer a request you've been praying about for a while.

God spoke through His prophet Elisha and told the men in a dry, hot desert to dig ditches all around the valley. God told them He would send water without the presence of strong winds, rain, or a storm. Despite being hot, thirsty, and probably tired, the men obeyed, and they prepared for the promise of water by digging the ditches. Note that God never gives us a promise without us having to work for it. This is demonstrated throughout the Bible. He gave people land, but they had to drive out their enemies to own it. He promised healing to people, but there was always something they had to do in obedience to receive it.

This scripture goes on to say that *suddenly* water flowed from the mountains and the land was filled with water. What would have happened if the men had said "No, God. It's too hot. We're too tired. Where will the water come from anyway?" What if the men were lazy and dug only one ditch instead of many? Their blessings would have flowed right past them!

While you are praying, speaking, and waiting, God wants you to be digging. Some of your blessings are going to come suddenly, friend! He is telling you to prepare for your blessings. Although they were hot and thirsty, the men were quite capable of digging the ditches. God will never require you to do anything outside of your abilities. He will ask you to do what He knows you are capable of doing so you can receive the blessing. Nineteenth century preacher Charles Spurgeon said, "If we expect to obtain the Holy Spirit's blessing, we must prepare for his reception."

I want to speak a word over you because I feel in my spirit that God is going to send some *suddenly* blessings your way! Someone is going to get a promotion, *suddenly*! Someone is going to discover their purpose, *suddenly*! Someone is going to be healed, *suddenly*! A debt is going to be canceled, *suddenly*! A credit score is going to increase, *suddenly*! A loved one is going to turn around for the better, *suddenly*! Business is going to boom, *suddenly*! You're going to meet the love of your life, *suddenly*! That marriage is going to be completely restored, *suddenly*! Those unhealthy strongholds and relationships are going to be broken, *suddenly*! The last part of today's scripture says it's suddenly to us, but it's a simple matter to God. In other words, He's like: "It's nothing. I'm God!"

Purpose Prayer for Today

Thank You, Lord, for my *suddenly* blessing that's on the way! I know some blessings are for an appointed time, but I believe there is a surprise with my name on it. Thank you Lord that the way you want me to prepare is not out of my reach. Give me the strength, the strategy, and the instructions on how to dig my ditches. Show me what that looks like for me. Lord, even when I am tired or when Your instructions don't make sense, help me to remember these men in the desert. The men didn't try to figure out how You would do it; they just obeyed. Today I choose to simply obey. No matter how weird, confusing, or incomprehensible your command is, I am going to prepare for my promises and receive my overflow. In Jesus's name, Amen.

Day 21

How can you prepare for the promises of God? If He sends overflow today, abundance today, more than enough today, will you have enough ditches to catch it all? What type of mindset and attitude do you think is necessary as you wait for your *suddenly* blessings?

_____
_____
_____
_____
_____
_____
_____
_____
_____
_____

Daily Affirmation: I am next in line for a suddenly blessing. I am well prepared and equipped to receive the things God has for me.

Day 22 Prayer

"I know that You can do everything, and that no purpose of Yours can be withheld from You." —Job 42:2, NKJV

Purpose in Your Pain

Today's word is just the most refreshing and reassuring scripture. Let's read that again. *"I know that You can do everything, and that no purpose of Yours can be withheld from You."* Job was a man tried and tested to the max. I don't know of anyone who was tried like Job. After losing all his children, being infected in his physical body, and having family and friends turn against him, He still said, "God I know Your purpose for my life cannot be stopped."

Many of us have been *through it*. From childhood to adulthood, life has been hard. We have all suffered loss, sickness, tragedy, and tough times. God never ever promised life would be easy. Instead, He assured us we *will* have trials in this world. But the beauty is that, despite what you've been through, your God-given purpose remains intact. Once God decides His purpose for your life, it's a done deal. In fact, the challenges and the hard times contribute to your purpose and who you will become.

I want to let you know God *will* accomplish His plans for you. I want you to take a moment to revisit your hard times. Although it hurts, try to dig out what you gained from those experiences.

When my mom died, I thought my life was over. I didn't even think I could make it. I watched her suddenly and unexpectedly pass on from this life to eternal life, and the last word that came out of her mouth was "Arika?" as if she was asking me what was happening.

As I write this with a lump in my throat now, I want you to understand *in losing the biggest part of me, I gained the biggest part of me.* I was mad at God. I hurt. I wasn't ready to lose her. Lord knows I still needed her. *But He never left me, and His purpose for me was not undone. It was uncovered.* I am who I am today because God didn't allow my pain, my anger, my hurt, or my confusion to stop what He was going to do with me and through me. It made me, it helped me, and it strengthened me. Friend, there is *purpose in your pain*. God knows what He is doing. Just survive it and live to tell your story because your story will help other people in theirs.

Purpose Prayer for Today

My God, thank You for not leaving me, for giving me space and room to hurt and be angry. Thank You for understanding my feelings but not allowing my feelings to interfere with Your purpose for me. It still hurts sometimes, God. I still wish some things were different. But I choose to trust You. I know You love me, and I know You got me. What can I say God? *My pain pushes me toward my purpose*, and for that I still have to say thank You. I've made up in my mind that no matter how much life hurts, I will not stop pushing. My pain and my experiences will help someone else with theirs. Like Job said, You can do everything God. So here I am; in spite of my pain, in spite of my trials, use me. In Jesus's name, Amen.

Day 22

Examine some of your most painful experiences in your life? In retrospect, what did you gain from them? If you're going through pain now, write out a list of things you think you can gain from it (e.g., strength, long-suffering, patience, trust, etc.). Now, how can you help others who have gone through similar struggles?

_____
_____
_____
_____
_____
_____
_____
_____
_____
_____

Daily Affirmation: I am not paralyzed by my pain. I am pushing toward my purpose in spite of the pain. My story will help someone else get through their pain, and therefore, it is not in vain.

Day 23 Prayer

When the angel of the Lord appeared to Gideon, he said, "The Lord is with you, you mighty warrior." The Lord turned to him and said, "Go in the strength you have and save Israel out of Midian's hand. Am I not sending you?" "Pardon me, my lord," Gideon replied, "but how can I save Israel? My clan is the weakest in Manasseh, and I am the least in my family." —Judges 6:12,14-15 NIV

What's My Name?

Gideon was a seemingly ordinary man. He was working in the winepress one day when God came and told him to go save the people of Israel. When God approached Gideon, He called him a mighty warrior. Gideon responded, "Umm, Lord, pardon me, but do you see who I am? Do you see where I come from? I am from the weakest clan, and I am the least of the weakest." In Judges 6:16, God responded by essentially saying, "I will be with you, and you will defeat the Midianites."

I want you to use your imagination for minute.

Imagine yourself sitting at work when God appears. Back then, it seemed pretty normal for God to show up without people flipping out, so let's pretend you don't lose it and you keep your cool. And God says, "Hey, *Insert you name here*, you president, you CEO, you motivational speaker, you great author, you millionaire." Whatever name He calls you by, you look around, behind you, and over at the next cubicle like "God, now I know You are not talking to me! Do you know where I'm from? I'm from the hood. I'm from a family of dropouts. I have a record. What do you mean *president*? I know you're not calling me a great author when I barely passed twelfth-grade English? I know you aren't calling me a motivational speaker when I'm depressed? I know you didn't just say millionaire when this job barely pays my bills? I know you don't expect me to open a day care when I'm a single mom? I know you don't expect me to counsel people when I grew up in foster care?

God's reply to you is the exact reply He gave to Gideon. *I will be with you, and you will!* Final answer. God doesn't care where you are from or what your family history is. He doesn't care if no one else has ever done it in your family. His concern is *you*. He called Gideon by the name He knew him by, mighty warrior. God often changed a person's name in the Bible. Gideon didn't feel mighty, and he certainly didn't see himself as a warrior, but God knew him. Remember day 1: *He already knew you!*

You are not defined by your past, where you are from, what you lack, or what you have. You are to answer to the name God calls you by. Gideon's purpose was to fight for the people of Israel and deliver them from their enemies. To do that, he had to answer to the name God called him by. If God is not limited by your background, please don't limit yourself. Your purpose is connected to the name He calls you. Answer the call God has on your life, and *fight* to walk in your purpose! While you are looking around and asking, "Who me?" God is looking at you and saying, "Yeah, you!" "God doesn't call the qualified. He qualifies the called" –Unknown

Purpose Prayer for Today

Father God, thank You that You know my real name! Thank You that I am not defined by my history or my background, but I am defined by who You call me. Thank You that *even when I question who I am, it doesn't change who I am.* Help me to not only accept the name You call me by, but also to know what that name is. I know the name my mother gave me, God, but what name do You give me? Give me ears that hear You and a mind and heart to comprehend You. Give me the courage to accept the call You have over my life. I declare today I will answer when You call me. I won't be afraid, and I won't be ashamed because You promise to be with me. In Jesus's name, Amen.

Day 23

How do you see yourself in this season of life? Have the names you've labeled yourself with lined up with the names God calls you? In what ways can you stand more firmly in your identity? God has called you by name to fulfill His purpose on earth. Are you willing to answer to that name?

_____

_____

_____

_____

_____

_____

_____

_____

_____

_____

_____

Daily Affirmation: I am a child of God. I answer to the names He calls me by. I am a mighty warrior. I am fearfully and wonderfully made. I will do all things through Christ who gives me strength.

Day 24 Prayer

And the Lord said to Gideon, "The people who are with you are too many for Me to give the Midianites into their hands, lest Israel claim glory for itself against Me, saying 'My own hand has saved me.'" —Judges 7:2, NKJV

What Is the Number?

I wanted to continue with Gideon today and show you something connected to yesterday's word. Before Gideon finally accepted his call to fight for Israel, he asked God for a sign to confirm His word, and God gave him a sign. (Side note: There's nothing wrong with asking God for a sign or for confirmation of what He said. I think that's wise, especially if you are not sure.) Gideon had gathered an army of over 22,000 men to go to war. But God told Gideon that He didn't want all those soldiers because they would think they won the battle on their own without Him. They went through a process of elimination, and reduced the army to a mere 300 men. Who do you think won the battle? The 300 men God had chosen of course!

Most of us have heard the saying "numbers don't lie." That might apply to the standards of the world, but based on what I know about God, all it takes is *one*. God didn't need an army of 22,000 when He was the one giving the victory. He didn't want the people to think they won the war because they had a huge army. No, they won because they had a *huge God*. It's not what you know; it's who you know.

God wants you to know all it takes is Him in your corner for you to win. You don't need any favors or handouts from anyone. He will bless you and use who He wants to use on your behalf.

I want you to have a "So what?" attitude. So what if your business started off small? So what if you don't have many connections? So what if this is your first time trying to discover your purpose? So what if you don't have the letters behind your name to get the job? All it takes is the right person, the right break, and the right move of God to change your life forever.

God wants the glory in your life. Don't let the world trick you into thinking that because the numbers look good, they are winning. That's not true. You win when you have the right *one* in your corner, *and that One is our Lord and Savior.*

Purpose Prayer for Today

Lord God, Thank You so much for being the only *one* I need. Thank You that my success and my blessings are not measured by the standards of the world but by You. Thank You that You can do more with less than I could do with my all. Lord, help me not to get caught up in numbers and logistics. You are my God, and I am Your child, and You always look out for Yours. Help me not to be intimidated or discouraged because of how things look on the outside. You are my inside man, pulling strings for me. Help me to remember that. I trust Your word, God. You plus me is the majority! What a mighty God I serve! In Jesus's name, Amen.

Day 24

Do you ever doubt your ability or your purpose because you don't feel well known? Have you ever found yourself getting caught up in numbers? Now that you know all you need is the One, who is God, by your side, how are you willing to show up in the world?

_____
_____
_____
_____
_____
_____
_____
_____
_____
_____
_____

Daily Affirmation: I have who I need to do everything I was born to do. With God by my side, there are no limits. Every battle I fight ends in victory because of the one who died for me.

Day 25 Prayer

Whoever watches the wind will not plant; whoever looks at the clouds will not reap. As you do not know the path of the wind, or how the body is formed in a mother's womb, so you cannot understand the work of God, the Maker of all things. Sow your seed in the morning and at evening let your hands not be idle, for you do not know which will succeed, whether this or that, or whether both will do equally well. —Ecclesiastes 11:4-6, NIV

Don't Put All Your Eggs in One Basket

I've heard two sayings which, in my opinion, contradict each other. One saying is: "Don't put all your eggs in one basket." The other saying is that you don't want to be a "Jack-of-all-trades and a master of none." So which one is it?

Let's break down today's word to see if we can find a happy medium. Solomon initially says that whoever is staring at the wind and looking up at the clouds will neither plant nor reap, so they will get no results. He goes on to say that we don't know from which direction the wind blows; we just feel it. We don't know how the amazing process of birth really works; as mothers, we just experience it. We don't even try to figure those things out. We just accept them for what they are. He is telling us we won't always understand how God does something. We just have to accept it for what it is.

Now here's where I really want to focus. Solomon says, "Sow your seed in the morning and at evening let not your hands be idle." To me, the happy medium is found here. We know that we can't do *nothing* and expect *something*. But I would argue he tells us we should *at least* be doing two things. Why two? Because you don't know which will succeed or if you will be successful with both.

Here's the harder question: *What* two things should you be doing?

Purpose evolves. It's big, but it can start off in one area and grow. Some of us work a day job by morning and a side hustle by night. For some of us, our purpose is outside of our workplace, but we must do *both* until our purpose evolves enough to sustain us. For others, maybe your purpose is in your workplace. *Walking in purpose doesn't automatically mean entrepreneurship. Some people find their calling in their careers.* But I would argue you shouldn't put all your confidence and stock into one job. Unfortunately, people lose their jobs every day with nothing to fall back on. Even if part of your purpose is in the workplace, doing something outside of that allows you to have something to fall back on. That doesn't always mean a financial safety net either. Volunteering or advocating for a cause you are passionate about can be a great fall back to keep you from sitting idle and staring at the clouds.

As long as you are actively pursuing purpose, actively doing something for the greater good, one or both will succeed. You don't know how God could bless you in the workplace, in your business, or even in your volunteering or advocating. It's not up to you to figure out the how; you must be obedient and *do*. Because when God is in it, success is inevitable! If you struggle with your job and how it aligns with your purpose, check out my blog post "Trapped vs. Assigned: Is Your Job from Heaven or Hell?" at shepursuespurpose.com/assigned.)

Purpose Prayer for Today

Father God, thank You that I'm not limited to one thing. Thank You that I can pursue my purpose whether I am in the workplace or not. Thank You for Your sovereignty. Thank You for Your ability to work things out for the good beyond human knowledge. Lord, I ask that you help me figure out what I should be doing to ensure I am not staring at the clouds and wasting time. Pull out my gifts, talents, and passions. Point me in the direction of my heart matters. I understand my purpose will evolve and grow as I evolve and grow. Today I declare I will try out new things. I will test the waters. I will continuously explore myself until I discover all the things I am called to do. In Jesus's name, Amen.

Day 25

Do you feel your purpose is connected to your career or to something else? What two areas that you are passionate about could you begin to work in? When do you feel most alive, energetic, and passionate?

_____
_____
_____
_____
_____
_____
_____
_____
_____
_____

Daily Affirmation: I am multi-gifted. God has not limited my abilities to serve and make a difference. Whether on my job, volunteering, or in my business, I am changing lives.

Day 26 Prayer

Now a certain man was there who had an infirmity thirty-eight years. When Jesus saw him . . . He said to him, "Do you want to be made well?' The sick man answered Him, "Sir, I have no man to put me into the pool when the water is stirred up; but while I am coming, another steps down before me." Jesus said to him "Rise, take up your bed and walk." —John 5:5-8, NKJV

How Bad Do You Want It?

I love this story about the sick man who was healed at the pool of Bethesda. He had struggled with a sickness that obviously had him paralyzed for almost four decades. A miracle of sorts would occur at this pool when it was stirred. The person who dipped their foot in first would be healed. When Jesus met this man, he had been attempting to get healed for a long time. When Jesus saw him, He went straight to the point. He didn't ask any leading questions. He didn't ask for the man's background or history. He didn't even say hello. He said, "Do you want to be made well?"

Why did Jesus ask him that? Wasn't it obvious the man had been trying to get healed at this pool? Furthermore, Jesus already knew the answer to the question, so why ask? I believe He wanted the man to answer because He wanted him to answer with faith. Jesus knows some people want to talk about how bad things are, but they're not willing to do anything to change their situation.

The man replied by saying, "Look. I've been trying to get into that pool, but everybody keeps beating me to the punch." I don't know about you, sis, but I heard excuses and self-pity in that response. He could have simply said, "Yes. Yes, I do want to be healed if You don't mind." Even after his response, Jesus didn't say, "Son, I'm so sorry other people wanted it more than you, so they went for it. I'm so sorry it has been so hard for you for thirty-eight years." Instead, Jesus responded with a command filled with love. He said "Rise, take up your bed and walk." And just like that, the man got up and was healed.

Although there is no divine pool for us to sit at, I think many of us can relate to this sick man. At one point or another in our lives, we've allowed an excuse, however valid it may have been, to keep us from getting up and walking in purpose. I told the story about how bad it hurt to lose my mom. That would've been a good enough excuse to sit for thirty-eight years, right?

God already knows everything about you. He already knows your condition and situation. His question to you is: *How bad do you want it though?* Whatever that *it* is, are you willing to do what it takes to get *it*? God is telling you that you don't have to wait decades or even years. You can get it now! Don't wait, don't make excuses, and don't let people stop you. It's time to *pursue*!

Purpose Prayer for Today

Father God, thank You for how patient You have been with me. Thank You that even though I may be off to a slow start, I am now in position to take up my bed and walk. I will not depend on anyone else to do for me what You are able to do for me. I will not make excuses; I will not let my past or my present hinder me from moving forward. Lord, everything I asked you for, *I want it bad*! I want it bad enough to work for it, fight for it, pray for it, and believe You for it. I declare today that *I will not give up. I will not give in. I will not settle!* I will walk in purpose, victory, love, joy, peace, prosperity, and all you have for me! In Jesus's name, Amen.

Day 26

What part of your life has paralyzed you? What has happened in the past that still stops you in your steps? What excuse are you making that blocks you from your healing? Single parenting? Not enough money? No support? Not enough resources? Bad childhood? What limiting belief keeps you stuck outside the pool?

_____
_____
_____
_____
_____
_____
_____
_____
_____
_____

Daily Affirmation: I am free, I am healed, and I am liberated. I am not paralyzed because I am pursuing my purpose. I am not an excuse maker because I am a move maker.

Day 27 Prayer

I can do all things through Christ who strengthens me.
—Philippians 4:13 NKJV

Let's Get Ready to Rumble!

Friend, you have come this far in this devotional because you are serious and committed to pursuing your purpose. And let me tell you, *the devil will do everything he can to throw you off course.* If he can't directly get at you, he will go after your marriage, your kids, your finances, or your emotions. He will go after whatever matters to you. But I want you to dig your heels in the ground and say, "I can do all things through Christ who gives me strength."

Expect trouble, expect pain, expect confusion, and expect disruptions when you walk in purpose. In the midst of expecting those things, *expect God to give you the strength to get through them!* Deuteronomy 33:25 (NKJV) says, "As your days are, so shall your strength be." God will give you whatever measure of strength you need to get through each day.

Next to football, I love boxing, and I have more than one favorite boxer. For instance, I have observed Deontay Wilder's style and perspective. Often times, per the score board, he's not winning most of the rounds. Historically, the opponent seemingly has the victory, until they make one wrong move and—whop!—he catches them off guard, and he knocks them out! His motto is: "They have to be perfect for twelve rounds to win. I only have to be perfect for two seconds." He's confident in his strength. He knows all it takes is the right combination and down goes the opponent. During a fight, boxers are taking hits. They are bobbing and weaving, but they are always calculating, always waiting for the moment to use their strength. I love it!

Boxers have strength, but so do we. Often, we don't even realize how much strength we have. Look back at all the things you've overcome so far. Losing your loved ones didn't kill you. Losing a job didn't stop you. Being lied on, lied to, cheated on, and misunderstood didn't make you throw in the towel. You didn't roll over and die when life kept punching you.

Life is like a boxing ring. You're going to take some hits and you will have to bob, weave, and calculate. In the movie *Creed*, Adonis Creed, played by Michael B. Jordan, was knocked down, and his corner told him to stay down for a few seconds. He stayed down to catch his breath and gather his strength. When he got back up, he was ready to finish, and he won. You can do the same thing. Keep bobbing and weaving. You're going take some hits, but stay in the ring. Stay down to gather your strength, but get up swinging. Christ is your two-second power punch. The enemy doesn't stand a chance against you!

Purpose Prayer for Today

Father God, thank You for being the *ultimate trainer* in this fight called life. Thank You that You are in my corner, giving me strength. Thank You that even when the enemy thinks he has me down, I have a two-second power punch he will never see coming. Thank You that every punch the devil lands just positions me to fight back. Lord, I'm tightening up my gloves today. I'm ready for the fight. I know You will give me the victory. I'm serving the devil notice. Satan, you are a liar and a loser, and you are going down for the count. I am a child of the King! No weapon formed against me shall prosper! No one can stop me. *I can do all things through Christ!* Let's gets ready to rumble. In Jesus's name, Amen.

Day 27

Have you ever felt like life has beaten you up? In what moments were you ready to throw in the towel? What kept you going? What motivated you to stay in the ring? What is the source of your strength? Are you committed to staying in the ring no matter how hard life gets?

_____
_____
_____
_____
_____
_____
_____
_____
_____
_____
_____
_____

Daily Affirmation: I am fighting *from* a place of victory, not *for* victory. God has already equipped me with the strength I need to fight. I am more than a conqueror.

Day 28 Prayer

And we know that all things work together for good to those who love God, to those who are the called according to His purpose. —Romans 8:28 NKJV

A Recipe for You

Sis, put on your cute lil' apron and let's go to the kitchen today. First, we are going to make a cake.

Mama's Vanilla Pound Cake

Ingredients

2 teaspoons of vanilla extract

1/2 pound (2 sticks) butter, plus more for pan

1/2 cup vegetable shortening

3 cups sugar

5 eggs

1 cup milk

3 cups all-purpose flour, plus more for pan

1/2 teaspoon fine salt

1/2 teaspoon baking powder

Preheat oven to 350 degrees. Mix the cream butter and shortening all together. Add sugar, a little at a time. Add eggs, 1 at a time. Stir dry ingredients together in a bowl and add to mixer alternately with milk, starting with the flour and ending with the flour. Mix in vanilla. Pour into a greased and floured tube pan and bake for 1 to 1 1/2 hours, until a toothpick inserted in the center of the cake comes out clean.

Now before you mix all the ingredients according to the instructions, I want you to crack open an egg yolk and drink it. Too nasty? Okay. How about licking a spoon filled with baking powder? Gross? How about sipping on three cups of sugar? Too sweet? How about a little salt then?

Here's where I'm going with this. When you try to eat these ingredients individually, they don't taste good, do they? Experienced in isolation, they are less than pleasant. But what happens when you mix them all up and put them in the oven? Its turns out to be a delicious dessert.

Here's another recipe.

Daddy's 8:28 Purpose Cake by The Trinity

Ingredients

*1 teaspoon of **disappointment***

*5 tablespoons of **crying tears***

*3 cups of **defeat***

*1 cup of **doubt***

1/2 teaspoon of **heartbreak**

1/2 pound of **sickness**

1/2 teaspoon of **sleepless nights**

1/2 cup of *fear*

3 sticks of **lost loved ones**

Preheat your heart and mind with the Word of God. Take disappointment, sickness, and fear, and mix them together. Slowly add lost loved ones to the mix, one at a time, and sprinkle crying tears over them. Crack heartbreak into the bowl. Finally, stir in sleepless nights and defeat. Put this mix in the fiery furnace called life. When the timer goes off, remove from the heat. Smell it. Although it's been in the fire, God promises it won't smell like smoke. Let it cool and indulge in the good 8:28 Cake God has for you!

Friend, this recipe is my metaphor for my favorite scripture in the Bible. When experienced separately, so many of the ingredients of life are terrible. They taste horrible, and we would rather go without. But if even one of those ingredients were missing, the recipe would be ruined. *All these things work together for our good.* It's hard to look forward to the final product when the individual ingredients suck, but Romans 8:28 assures us our chef called Christ wouldn't have given you the ingredients if it wasn't going to turn out good. Don't throw away the recipe before it's done, sis. God has something cooking in the kitchen for you, and when it's done, it's going to taste oh so good!

Purpose Prayer for Today

Dear God, Thank You that the good, the bad, and the ugly all work together for my good. Thank You that when You are in it, nothing happens by chance or accident. Thank You that everything I have gone through and will go through has been divinely inspected by You first. There is nothing in the mix that will poison or harm me. Lord, help me to remember your 8:28 recipe. When life gets hard, help me to remember it's just one ingredient, not the final product. Your word says I am called according to Your purpose. I receive that and I declare I will keep cooking until it is finished. I will not leave the kitchen too soon or when the furnace gets too hot. I command every ingredient of life to get in alignment with Your calling and purpose for my life. In Jesus's name, Amen.

Day 28

What are some ingredients of life you've experienced that haven't tasted so good? What moments made you think life was over? In retrospect, how did God work that out for your good? What are you experiencing now that you believe will work out for the good?

_____
_____
_____
_____
_____
_____
_____
_____
_____
_____
_____

Daily Affirmation: I am full of good things. Everything I have been through has deposited something good in me. All things I have experienced work together for my good.

Day 29 Prayer

"Martha, Martha," the Lord answered, "You are worried and upset about many things, but few things are needed—or indeed only one. Mary has chosen what is better, and it will not be taken away from her."
—Luke 10:41-42 NIV

The Chosen One

Do you remember the two sisters Mary and Martha? Jesus came into their village, and Martha invited Him into her home. When He arrived, Martha immediately got to work. The Bible says she was distracted with much serving. Her sister, Mary, decided to sit at Jesus's feet to listen to what He was saying. As Martha was busy serving, she looked to Jesus and said "Lord, do you not care that my sister has left me alone to serve?" Today's word gives us Jesus's response.

Many of us can relate to Martha. Who wouldn't want to serve Jesus, the King, in their home? I believe Martha had the right idea but made the wrong choice. Jesus even told Martha that Mary had *chosen* what was better.

Here's what I want you to see. Jesus didn't command Martha to get busy with serving, nor did He command Mary to sit as His feet. They were both given a choice. Although most women are tasked with many to-dos and much serving, we always have a choice. The key is to discern the *right thing* versus the *good thing*. It was good that Martha decided to serve her Savior in her home. But in that moment, the right thing to do was to be served by Jesus. Mary made the right decision, the better decision in that moment.

As you pursue your purpose, as you aim to carry out your calling, you must constantly evaluate and assess the few things that are needed. Know and understand that, in spite of all the things you have to do, the one thing that remains a priority is sitting at your Savior's feet. When you prioritize your time with Jesus, He can give you a daily strategy for all the other things you have to do.

For many of us, there don't seem to be enough hours in the day to get all the things done that need to be done. Allowing Him to help us focus on a few things enables us to be more productive and effective throughout our day. Paul said it best when he said, "I have the right (*or choice*) to do anything, but not everything is beneficial" (1 Corinthian, 10:23 NIV).

Purpose Prayer for Today

Father God, thank You for the gift of choice. Thank You for providing options and opportunities for me. Lord, I ask from this day forward You help me to make the right decisions in my everyday life. Help me to know the few things that are needed each day. More importantly, help me to prioritize the one thing that will always be needed—spending time with You. Help me to remember that, as I sit at Your feet, You will give me the daily strategies I need to feel accomplished and productive. Lord, I ask for a spirit of discernment. I am responsible for many things. Show me each day which are worth my time and energy. Show me the things that are beneficial. I trust You and commit my plans to You. In Jesus's name, Amen.

Day 29

Which sister, Martha or Mary, do you relate to best? Are you often busy and distracted with much serving? How often do you make time to sit at Jesus's feet? How does today's devotional impact the choices you'll make moving forward? What do you plan to do differently?

_____

_____

_____

_____

_____

_____

_____

_____

_____

_____

Daily Affirmation: I no longer allow myself to be distracted with much serving. I sit at my Savior's feet first, and I allow Him to give me the daily strategies I need to carry out above everything else.

Day 30 Prayer

My determined purpose is that I may know Him, that I may progressively become more deeply acquainted with Him, perceiving and recognizing and understanding the wonders of His Person. —Philippians 3:10, AMPC

To Know Him Is to Love Him

Sis, guess what! I know what your purpose is! Well, part of it anyway. God has given us all a specific purpose and different gifts, but there is a universal purpose that applies to every single one of us, and that is *to know God and to make him known*. It seems so simple, and yet, it's so complex. When God created the world, His intent was for all of us to have a relationship with Him. We know the story of Adam and Eve and how they were deceived. Now we live in a world infected with darkness. That darkness, no matter what form it may come in, has made it hard for all of Creation to know God, which was His ultimate purpose. Those of us who are believers know that, despite what has taken place, there will come a day when His purpose is fulfilled.

In the Bible, God performed all kinds of miracles. He rewarded people, punished people, and used people in so many ways. No matter how He showed up, the common denominator was always the same. God would always say, "Then they will *know* that I am the Lord." That was always the motive behind His actions, and it still is today.

Friend, *God wants you to know that He loves you*. He really laid that in my spirit. Somehow, we think because we're not "living right," because we have some "habits," or because of some bad things we have done that He's giving us the silent treatment. No, God is not like us. His love for us is unconditional. He loves you with every breath you take. He already knows you, and He just wants you to know Him. *That is the #1 purpose of this life*. What's funny is the more you get to know Him (just like you know a friend or father) the more you love Him.

As we near the end of this book, I want you to keep this in mind. While you do have some specific kingdom work to do, God wants you to know Him. He wants a personal relationship with you. Loving Him comes automatically once you know Him, and no matter how much you already know about God, there is more to Him. The deeper you go the more He will show you who He is.

I challenge you today to pursue your #1 purpose first. You'll find that when you start with your primary purpose, the rest comes naturally. I'm telling you, friend, God is so strategic. He has handpicked you to read this book. This is a sign. This is God telling you through me that He wants you closer and wants to go deeper with you. I speak over you that this year is special for you. This year you will know Him like never before!

Purpose Prayer for Today

Father, Friend, Counselor, Daddy, God—there are so many names for who You can be, Lord. Thank You for Your ability to be whatever I need You to be at any given moment. Thank

You that You are not mad me, You are not disappointed in me, and You are not ashamed of me. Thank You, Lord, that there is *nothing* that can separate me from Your love. God, help me to love You back. Help me to get to know You better. Put that at the forefront of my heart and mind. Help me pursue my #1 purpose of knowing You first, and I know the rest will come easy. Help me to forgive myself. Sometimes I may hold my own shame and disappointment against You. I release that today. I am worthy of Your love. I deserve Your love. *I am enough.* Mistakes, scars, habits, failures, and all, *I am Yours and You are mine.* It may take me some time, and it will take practice, but Lord, *my predetermined purpose is to know you.* In Jesus's name, Amen.

Day 30

What is your relationship with God like? How well are you acquainted with Him and His word? What steps can you take to grow closer to Him no matter how close you are now? What practical habits will you need to develop to grow in your spiritual walk?

_____
_____
_____
_____
_____
_____
_____
_____
_____
_____
_____
_____
_____

Daily Affirmation: I am determined to know my God. It is my life's mission to make Him known.

A Letter to My Sister in Purpose

Dear Sister,

I would first like to thank you for investing in yourself by buying this book. It started out simply as a Pray for Purpose Challenge to grow my online community. However, God had other plans. These prayers have touched the spirits and souls of women in pursuit of purpose, and I pray they've done the same for you.

I want to end this book by speaking into your life. I want you to know God has a purpose for you bigger than you could ever imagine. I want you to know nothing you have gone through up to this very moment has been wasted. God is the master at working all things together for the good. As I mentioned in the introduction, you are pregnant with purpose. There's something growing on the inside of you, waiting to be birthed. Don't stop pushing even when things may be painful. Don't stop pursuing for fear of what others may so or do. Don't give up when it feels like everything is falling apart. Don't allow fear, procrastination, or doubt to paralyze you and keep you from walking in purpose.

Pursue, sis!

Don't allow mom guilt, wife guilt, or any guilt to trick you into thinking pursuing purpose is selfish. You were an individual, God's child, before you took on any other role. A specific group of people is assigned to you. They are waiting and need you to answer yes to the call. Don't be afraid to dream big, believe big, or make big moves. You serve a big God. Big is your portion, sis.

Unapologetically pursue, sis!

Be willing to invest in the person of purpose you are becoming. Be willing to take care of you while you take care of others. Be willing to sit at God's feet to get what He has for you. You were made for greatness. You are God's child, fearfully and wonderfully made, and He loves you. He is going to use you, and you are going to bring Him glory. Your mistakes, the setbacks, the delays—they don't define you. You are a woman of purpose, sis.

Relentlessly pursue your purpose, sis!

With love and prayers, your Sis in Purpose,

Arika Davenport

Join the Purpose Movement at shepursuespurpose.com

What Is My Purpose?

This is the most universally asked question. Every human has a deep desire to know why they were created. Everyone wants to know the true meaning of their life. No matter how it is expressed, every person wants to fulfill their dreams and live a life with purpose. For many, the problem is not knowing where to start or what steps to take.

Whether you know your purpose in life or you're in search of it, this *Prayers for Purpose* devotional journal is the guide that will help you obtain the clarity and direction you need to walk into your destiny. In this easy to read and apply devotional, Arika captures the thoughts, concerns, and dreams of every purpose-driven woman.

Conversations around purpose, faith, and destiny can sometimes be so spiritual that it's hard to apply them to everyday life. This book delivers prayers in a down-to-earth manner. The journal prompts and daily affirmations will stretch your thinking and encourage you to make adjustments that align with your vision. After reading this book, every woman will have the tools to pray, plan, and take action for her purpose!

www.ingramcontent.com/pod-product-compliance
Lightning Source LLC
Chambersburg PA
CBHW050913160426
43194CB00011B/2389